Lover's Vows

E. Inchbald

Lovers Vows

A Play in Five Acts

by

Mrs. Inchbald

from the German of Kotzebue

PREFACE.

IT would appear like affectation to offer an apology for any scenes or passages omitted or added, in this play, different from the original: its reception has given me confidence to suppose what I have done is right; for Kotzebue's "Child of Love" in Germany, was never more attractive than "Lovers' Vows" has been in England.

I could trouble my reader with many pages to disclose the motives which induced me to alter, with the exception of a few common-place sentences only, the characters of Count Cassel, Amelia, and Verdun the Butler—I could explain why the part of the Count, as in the original, would inevitably have condemned the whole Play, —I could inform my reader why I have pourtrayed the Baron in many particulars different from the German author, and carefully prepared the audience for the grand effect of the last scene in the fourth act, by totally changing his conduct towards his son as a robber—why I gave sentences of a humourous kind to the parts of the two Cottagers—why I was compelled, on many occasions, to compress the matter of a speech of three or four pages into one of three or four lines—and why, in no one instance, I would suffer my respect for Kotzebue to interfere with my profound respect for the judgment of a British audience. But I flatter myself such a vindication is not requisite to the enlightened reader, who, I trust, on comparing this drama with the original, will at once see all my motives—and the dull admirer of mere verbal translation, it would be vain to endeavour to inspire with taste by instruction.

Wholly unacquainted with the German language, a literal translation of the "Child of Love" was given to me by the manager of Covent Garden Theatre to be fitted, as my opinion should direct, for his stage. This translation, tedious and vapid as most literal translations are, had the peculiar disadvantage of having been put into our language by a German—of course it came to me in broken English. It was no slight misfortune to have an example of bad grammar, false metaphors and similes, with all the usual errors of feminine diction, placed before a female writer. But if, disdaining the construction of sentences, —the precise decorum of the cold grammarian, —she has caught the spirit of her author, —if, in every altered scene, —still adhering to the nice propriety of his meaning, and still keeping in view his great catastrophe, —she has agitated her audience with all the various passions he depicted, the rigid criticism of the closet will be but a slender abatement of the pleasure resulting from the sanction of an applauding theatre.

It has not been one of the least gratifications I have received from the success of this play, that the original German, from which it is taken, was printed in the year 1791; and yet, that during all the period which has intervened, no person of talents or literary knowledge (though there are in this country many of that description, who profess to search for German dramas) has thought it worth employment to make a translation of the work. I can only account for such an apparent neglect of Kotzebue's "Child of Love, " by the consideration of its original unfitness for an English stage, and the difficulty of making it otherwise—a difficulty which once appeared so formidable, that I seriously thought I must have declined it even after I had proceeded some length in the undertaking.

Independently of objections to the character of the Count, the dangerous insignificance of the Butler, in the original, embarrassed me much. I found, if he was retained in the *Dramatis Personae*, something more must be supplied than the author had assigned him: I suggested the verses I have introduced; but not being blessed with the Butler's happy art of rhyming, I am indebted for them, except the seventh and eleventh stanzas in the first of his poetic stories, to the author of the prologue.

The part of Amelia has been a very particular object of my solicitude and alteration: the same situations which the author gave her remain, but almost all the dialogue of the character I have changed: the forward and unequivocal manner in which she announces her affection to her lover, in the original, would have been revolting to an English audience: the passion of love, represented on the stage, is certain to be insipid or disgusting, unless it creates smiles or tears: Amelia's love, by Kotzebue, is indelicately blunt, and yet void of mirth or sadness: I have endeavoured to attach the attention and sympathy of the audience by whimsical insinuations, rather than coarse abruptness—the same woman, I conceive, whom the author drew, with the self-same sentiments, but with manners adapted to the English rather than the German taste; and if the favour in which this character is held by the audience, together with every sentence and incident which I have presumed to introduce in the play, may be offered as the criterion of my skill, I am sufficiently rewarded for the task I have performed.

In stating the foregoing circumstances relating to this production, I hope not to be suspected of arrogating to my own exertions only, the popularity which has attended "The Child of Love, " under the title of "Lovers' Vows, "—the exertions of every performer engaged in the play deservedly claim a share in its success; and I must sincerely thank them for the high importance of their aid.

PROLOGUE.

WRITTEN BY JOHN TAYLOR, ESQ.

SPOKEN BY Mr. MURRAY.

POETS have oft' declared, in doleful strain,
That o'er dramatic tracks they beat in vain,
Hopeless that novelty will spring to sight;
For life and nature are exhausted quite.
Though plaints like these have rung from age to age,
Too kind are writers to desert the stage;
And if they, fruitless, search for unknown prey,
At least they dress *old game a novel way*;
But such lamentings should be heard no more,
For modern taste turns Nature out of door;
Who ne'er again her former sway will boast,
Till, to complete her works, *she starts a ghost.*
   If such the mode, what can we hope to-night,
Who rashly dare approach without a sprite?
No dreadful cavern, no midnight scream,
No rosin flames, nor e'en one flitting gleam.
Nought of the charms so potent to invite
The monstrous charms of terrible delight.
Our present theme the German Muse supplies,
But rather aims to soften than surprise.
Yet, with her woes she strives some smiles to blend,
Intent as well to cheer as to amend:
On her own native soil she knows the art
To charm the fancy, and to touch the heart.
If, then, she mirth and pathos can express,
Though less engaging in an English dress,
Let her from British hearts no peril fear,
But, as a STRANGER*, find a welcome here.

* Hamlet.

DRAMATIS PERSONAE.

MEN.

BARON WILDENHAIM.	Mr. Murray.
COUNT CASSEL.	Mr. Knight.
ANHALT.	Mr. H. Johnston.
FREDERICK	Mr. Pope.
VERDUN the BUTLER	Mr. Munden.
LANDLORD.	Mr. Thompson.
COTTAGER.	Mr. Davenport.
FARMER.	Mr. Rees.
COUNTRYMAN.	Mr. Dyke.

Huntsmen, Servants, &c.

WOMEN.

AGATHA FRIBURG.	Mrs. Johnson.
AMELIA WILDENHAIM	Mrs. H. Johnston.
COTTAGER'S WIFE	Mrs. Davenport.
COUNTRY GIRL.	Miss Leserve.

SCENE, Germany—Time of representation one day.

ACT I.

SCENE I. A high road, a town at a distance—A small inn on one side of the road—A cottage on the other.

The LANDLORD of the inn leads AGATHA by the hand out of his house.

LANDLORD. No, no! no room for you any longer—It is the fair to-day in the next village; as great a fair as any in the German dominions. The country people with their wives and children take up every corner we have.

AGATHA. You will turn a poor sick woman out of doors who has spent her last farthing in your house.

LANDLORD. For that very reason; because she *has* spent her last farthing.

AGATHA. I can work.

LANDLORD. You can hardly move your hands.

AGATHA. My strength will come again.

LANDLORD. Then *you* may come again.

AGATHA. What am I to do? Where shall I go?

LANDLORD. It is fine weather—you may go any where.

AGATHA. Who will give me a morsel of bread to satisfy my hunger?

LANDLORD. Sick people eat but little.

AGATHA. Hard, unfeeling man, have pity.

LANDLORD. When times are hard, pity is too expensive for a poor man. Ask alms of the different people that go by.

AGATHA. Beg! I would rather starve.

LANDLORD. You may beg and starve too. What a fine lady you are! Many an honest woman has been obliged to beg. Why should not you? [Agatha sits down upon a large stone under a tree.] For instance, here comes somebody; and I will teach you how to begin. [A Countryman, with working tools, crosses the road.] Good day, neighbour Nicholas.

COUNTRYMAN. Good day. [Stops.]

LANDLORD. Won't you give a trifle to this poor woman? [Countryman takes no notice, but walks off.] That would not do— the poor man has nothing himself but what he gets by hard labour. Here comes a rich farmer; perhaps he will give you something.

Enter FARMER.

LANDLORD. Good morning to you, Sir. Under yon tree sits a poor woman in distress, who is in need of your charity.

FARMER. Is she not ashamed of herself? Why don't she work?

LANDLORD. She has had a fever. —If you would but pay for one dinner—

FARMER. The harvest has been indifferent, and my cattle and sheep have suffered distemper. [Exit.

LANDLORD. My fat, smiling face was not made for begging: you'll have more luck with your thin, sour one—so, I'll leave you to yourself. [Exit.

[Agatha rises and comes forward.]

AGATHA. Oh Providence! thou hast till this hour protected me, and hast given me fortitude not to despair. Receive my humble thanks, and restore me to health, for the sake of my poor son, the innocent cause of my sufferings, and yet my only comfort. [kneeling] Oh, grant that I may see him once more! See him improved in strength of mind and body; and that by thy gracious mercy he may never be visited with afflictions great as mine. [After a pause] Protect his father too, merciful Providence, and pardon his crime of perjury to me! Here, in the face of heaven (supposing my end approaching, and that I can but a few days longer struggle with want and sorrow), here, I solemnly forgive my seducer for all the ills, the accumulated evils which his allurements, his deceit, and cruelty, have for twenty years past drawn upon me.

> Enter a COUNTRY GIRL with a basket.

AGATHA [near fainting]. My dear child, if you could spare me a trifle—

GIRL. I have not a farthing in the world—But I am going to market to sell my eggs, and as I come back I'll give you three-pence—And I'll be back as soon as ever I can. [Exit.

AGATHA. There was a time when I was as happy as this country girl, and as willing to assist the poor in distress. [Retires to the tree and sits down.]

> Enter FREDERICK—He is dressed in a German soldier's
> uniform, has a knapsack on his shoulders, appears in
> high spirits, and stops at the door of the inn.

FREDERICK. Halt! Stand at ease! It is a very hot day—A draught of good wine will not be amiss. But first let me consult my purse. [Takes out a couple of pieces of money, which he turns about in his hand.] This will do for a breakfast—the other remains for my dinner; and in the evening I shall be home. [Calls out] Ha! Halloo! Landlord! [Takes notice of Agatha, who is leaning against the tree.] Who is that? A poor sick woman! She don't beg; but her appearance makes me think she is in want. Must one always wait to give till one is asked? Shall I go without my breakfast now, or lose my dinner? The first I think is best. Ay, I don't want a breakfast, for dinner time will soon be here. To do good satisfies both hunger and thirst. [Going towards her with the money in his hand.] Take this, good woman.

> [She stretches her hand for the gift, looks steadfastly at
> him, and cries out with astonishment and joy.]

AGATHA. Frederick!

FREDERICK. Mother! [With astonishment and grief.] Mother! For God's sake what is this! How is this! And why do I find my mother thus? Speak!

3

AGATHA. I cannot speak, dear son! [Rising and embracing him.] My dear Frederick! The joy is too great—I was not prepared—

FREDERICK. Dear mother, compose yourself: [leans her against his breast] now, then, be comforted. How she trembles! She is fainting.

AGATHA. I am so weak, and my head so giddy—I had nothing to eat all yesterday.

FREDERICK. Good heavens! Here is my little money, take it all! Oh mother! mother! [Runs to the inn]. Landlord! Landlord! [knocking violently at the door.]

LANDLORD. What is the matter?

FREDERICK. A bottle of wine—quick, quick!

LANDLORD [surprised]. A bottle of wine! For who?

FREDERICK. For me. Why do you ask? Why don't you make haste?

LANDLORD. Well, well, Mr. soldier: but can you pay for it?

FREDERICK. Here is money—make haste, or I'll break every window in your house.

LANDLORD. Patience! Patience! [goes off.

FREDERICK [to Agatha]. You were hungry yesterday when I sat down to a comfortable dinner. You were hungry when I partook of a good supper. Oh! Why is so much bitter mixed with the joy of my return?

AGATHA. Be patient, my dear Frederick. Since I see you, I am well. But I *have been* ill: so ill, that I despaired of ever beholding you again.

FREDERICK. Ill, and I was not with you? I will, now, never leave you more. Look, mother, how tall and strong I am grown. There arms can now afford you support. They can, and shall, procure you subsistence.

[Landlord coming out of the house with a small pitcher.]

LANDLORD. Here is wine—a most delicious nectar. [Aside.] It is only Rhenish; but it will pass for the best old Hock.

FREDERICK [impatiently snatching the pitcher]. Give it me.

LANDLORD. No, no—the money first. One shilling and two-pence, if you please.

[Frederick gives him money.]

FREDERICK. This is all I have. —Here, here, mother.

[While she drinks Landlord counts the money.]

LANDLORD. Three halfpence too short! However, one must be charitable. [Exit Landlord.

AGATHA. I thank you, my dear Frederick—Wine revives me—Wine from the hand of my son gives me almost a new life.

FREDERICK. Don't speak too much, mother. —Take your time.

AGATHA. Tell me, dear child, how you have passed the five years since you left me.

FREDERICK. Both good and bad, mother. To day plenty—to-morrow not so much—And sometimes nothing at all.

AGATHA. You have not written to me this long while.

FREDERICK. Dear mother, consider the great distance I was from you! —And then, in the time of war, how often letters miscarry. —Besides — —

AGATHA. No matter now I see you. But have you obtained your discharge?

FREDERICK. Oh, no, mother—I have leave of absence only for two months; and that for a particular reason. But I will not quit you so soon, now I find you are in want of my assistance.

AGATHA. No, no, Frederick; your visit will make me so well, that I shall in a very short time recover strength to work again; and you must return to your regiment when your furlough is expired. But you told me leave of absence was granted you for a particular reason. —What reason?

FREDERICK. When I left you five years ago, you gave me every thing you could afford, and all you thought would be necessary for me. But one trifle you forgot, which was, the certificate of my birth from the church-book. —You know in this country there is nothing to be done without it. At the time of parting from you, I little thought it could be of that consequence to me which I have since found it would have been. Once I became tired of a soldier's life, and in the hope I should obtain my discharge, offered myself to a master to learn a profession; but his question was, "Where is your certificate from the church-book of the parish in which you were born? " It vexed me that I had not it to produce, for my comrades laughed at my disappointment. My captain behaved kinder, for he gave me leave to come home to fetch it—and you see, mother, here I am.

[During this speech Agatha is confused and agitated.

AGATHA. So, you are come for the purpose of fetching your certificate from the church-book.

FREDERICK. Yes, mother.

AGATHA. Oh! oh!

FREDERICK. What is the matter? [She bursts into tears.] For heaven's sake, mother, tell me what's the matter?

AGATHA. You have no certificate.

FREDERICK. No!

AGATHA. No. —The laws of Germany excluded you from being registered at your birth—for—you are a natural son!

FREDERICK [starts—after a pause]. So! —And who is my father?

AGATHA. Oh Frederick, your wild looks are daggers to my heart. Another time.

FREDERICK [endeavouring to conceal his emotion]. No, no—I am still your son—and you are still my mother. Only tell me, who is my father?

AGATHA. When we parted five years ago, you were too young to be intrusted with a secret of so much importance. —But the time is come when I can, in confidence, open my heart, and unload that burthen with which it has been long oppressed. And yet, to reveal my errors to my child, and sue for his mild judgment on my conduct — —

FREDERICK. You have nothing to sue for; only explain this mystery.

AGATHA. I will, I will. But—my tongue is locked with remorse and shame. You must not look at me.

FREDERICK. Not look at you! Cursed be that son who could find his mother guilty, although the world should call her so.

AGATHA. Then listen to me, and take notice of that village, [pointing] of that castle, and of that church. In that village I was born—in that church I was baptized. My parents were poor, but reputable farmers. —The lady of that castle and estate requested them to let me live with her, and she would provide for me through life. They resigned me; and at the age of fourteen I went to my patroness. She took pleasure to instruct me in all kinds of female literature and accomplishments, and three happy years had passed under protection, when her only son, who was an officer in the Saxon service, obtained permission to come home. I had never seen him before—he was a handsome young man—in my eyes a prodigy; for he talked of love, and promised me marriage. He was the first man who ever spoken to me on such a subject. —His flattery made me vain, and his repeated vows—Don't look at me, dear Frederick! —I can say no more. [Frederick with his eyes cast down, takes her hand, and puts it to his heart.] Oh! oh! my son! I was intoxicated by the fervent caresses of a young, inexperienced, capricious man, and did not recover from the delirium till it was too late.

FREDERICK [after a pause]. Go on. —Let me know more of my father.

AGATHA. When the time drew near that I could no longer conceal my guilt and shame, my seducer prevailed upon me not to expose

7

him to the resentment of his mother. He renewed his former promises of marriage at her death; —on which relying, I gave him my word to be secret—and I have to this hour buried his name deep in my heart.

FREDERICK. Proceed, proceed! give me full information—I will have courage to hear it all. [Greatly agitated.]

AGATHA. His leave of absence expired, he returned to his regiment, depending on my promise, and well assured of my esteem. As soon as my situation became known, I was questioned, and received many severe reproaches: But I refused to confess who was my undoer; and for that obstinacy was turned from the castle. —I went to my parents; but their door was shut against me. My mother, indeed, wept as she bade me quit her sight for ever; but my father wished increased affliction might befall me.

FREDERICK [weeping]. Be quick with your narrative, or you'll break my heart.

AGATHA. I now sought protection from the old clergyman of the parish. He received me with compassion. On my knees I begged forgiveness for the scandal I had caused to his parishioners; promised amendment; and he said he did not doubt me. Through his recommendation I went to town; and hid in humble lodgings, procured the means of subsistence by teaching to the neighbouring children what I had learnt under the tuition of my benefactress. —- To instruct you, my Frederick, was my care and delight; and in return for your filial love I would not thwart your wishes when they led to a soldier's life: but my health declined, I was compelled to give up my employment, and, by degrees, became the object you now see me. But, let me add, before I close my calamitous story, that—when I left the good old clergyman, taking along with me his kind advice and his blessing, I left him with a firm determination to fulfil the vow I had made of repentance and amendment. I *have* fulfilled it— and now, Frederick, you may look at me again. [He embraces her.]

FREDERICK. But my father all this time? [mournfully] I apprehend he died.

AGATHA. No—he married.

FREDERICK. Married!

AGATHA. A woman of virtue—of noble birth and immense fortune. Yet, [weeps] I had written to him many times; had described your infant innocence and wants; had glanced obliquely at former promises—

FREDERICK [rapidly]. No answer to these letters?

AGATHA. Not a word. —But in time of war, you know, letters miscarry.

FREDERICK. Nor did he ever return to this estate?

AGATHA. No—since the death of his mother this castle has only been inhabited by servants—for he settled as far off as Alsace, upon the estate of his wife.

FREDERICK. I will carry you in my arms to Alsace. No—why should I ever know my father, if he is a villain! My heart is satisfied with a mother. —No—I will not go to him. I will not disturb his peace—O leave that task to his conscience. What say you, mother, can't we do without him? [Struggling between tears and his pride.] We don't want him. I will write directly to my captain. Let the consequence be what it will, leave you again I cannot. Should I be able to get my discharge, I will work all day at the plough, and all the night with my pen. It will do, mother, it will do! Heaven's goodness will assist me—it will prosper the endeavours of a dutiful son for the sake of a helpless mother.

AGATHA [presses him to her breast]. Where could be found such another son?

FREDERICK. But tell me my father's name, that I may know how to shun him.

AGATHA. Baron Wildenhaim.

FREDERICK. Baron Wildenhaim! I shall never forget it. —Oh! you are near fainting. Your eyes are cast down. What's the matter? Speak, mother!

AGATHA. Nothing particular. —Only fatigued with talking. I wish to take a little rest.

FREDERICK. I did not consider that we have been all this time in the open road. [Goes to the Inn, and knocks at the door.] Here, Landlord!

LANDLORD re-enters.

LANDLORD. Well, what is the matter now?

FREDERICK. Make haste, and get a bed ready for this good woman.

LANDLORD [with a sneer]. A bed for this good woman! ha, ha ha! She slept last night in that pent-house; so she may to-night. [Exit, shutting door.

FREDERICK. You are an infamous—[goes back to his mother] Oh! my poor mother—[runs to the Cottage at a little distance, and knocks]. Ha! hallo! Who is there?

Enter COTTAGER.

COTTAGER. Good day, young soldier. —What is it you want?

FREDERICK. Good friend, look at that poor woman. She is perishing in the public road! It is my mother. —Will you give her a small corner in your hut? I beg for mercy's sake—Heaven will reward you.

COTTAGER. Can't you speak quietly? I understand you very well. [Calls at the door of the hut.] Wife, shake up our bed—here's a poor sick woman wants it. [Enter WIFE]. Why could not you say all this in fewer words? Why such a long preamble? Why for mercy's sake, and heaven's reward? Why talk about reward for such trifles as these? Come, let us lead her in; and welcome she shall be to a bed, as good as I can give her; and our homely fare.

FREDERICK. Ten thousand thanks, and blessings on you!

WIFE. Thanks and blessings! here's a piece of work indeed about nothing! Good sick lady, lean on my shoulder. [To Frederick] Thanks and reward indeed! Do you think husband and I have lived to these years, and don't know our duty? Lean on my shoulder. [Exeunt into the Cottage.

END ACT I.

ACT II.

SCENE I. A room in the cottage.

AGATHA, COTTAGER, his WIFE, and FREDERICK discovered—
AGATHA reclined upon a wooden bench, FREDERICK leaning over
her.

FREDERICK. Good people have you nothing to give her? Nothing
that's nourishing.

WIFE. Run, husband, run, and fetch a bottle of wine from the
landlord of the inn.

FREDERICK. No, no—his wine is as bad as his heart: she has drank
some of it, which I am afraid has turned to poison.

COTTAGER. Suppose, wife, you look for a new-laid egg?

WIFE. Or a drop of brandy, husband—that mostly cures me.

FREDERICK. Do you hear, mother—will you, mother? [Agatha
makes a sign with her hand as if she could not take any thing.] She
will not. Is there no doctor in this neighbourhood?

WIFE. At the end of the village there lives a horse-doctor. I have
never heard of any other.

FREDERICK. What shall I do? She is dying. My mother is dying. —
Pray for her, good people!

AGATHA. Make yourself easy, dear Frederick, I am well, only
weak—Some wholesome nourishment—

FREDERICK. Yes, mother, directly—directly. [Aside] Oh where shall
I—no money—not a farthing left.

WIFE. Oh, dear me! Had you not paid the rent yesterday, husband—

COTTAGER. I then, should know what to do. But as I hope for
mercy, I have not a penny in my house.

FREDERICK. Then I must—[Apart, coming forward]—Yes, I will go, and beg. —But should I be refused—I will then—I leave my mother in your care, good people—Do all you can for her, I beseech you! I shall soon be with you again. [Goes off in haste and confusion.]

COTTAGER. If he should go to our parson, I am sure he would give him something.

> [Agatha having revived by degrees during the scene, rises.]

AGATHA. Is that good old man still living, who was minister here some time ago?

WIFE. No—It pleased Providence to take that worthy man to heaven two years ago. —We have lost in him both a friend and a father. We shall never get such another.

COTTAGER. Wife, wife, our present rector is likewise a very good man.

WIFE. Yes! But he is so very young.

COTTAGER. Our late parson was once young too.

WIFE [to Agatha.] This young man being tutor in our Baron's family, he was very much beloved by them all; and so the Baron gave him this living in consequence.

COTTAGER. And well he deserved it, for his pious instructions to our young lady: who is, in consequence, good, and friendly to every body.

AGATHA. What young lady do you mean?

COTTAGER. Our Baron's daughter.

AGATHA. Is she here?

WIFE. Dear me! Don't you know that? I thought every body had known that. It is almost five weeks since the Baron and all his family arrived at the castle.

AGATHA. Baron Wildenhaim?

WIFE. Yes, Baron Wildenhaim.

AGATHA. And his lady?

COTTAGER. His lady died in France many miles from hence, and her death, I suppose, was the cause of his coming to this estate—For the Baron has not been here till within these five weeks ever since he was married. We regretted his absence much, and his arrival has caused great joy.

WIFE [addressing her discourse to Agatha.] By all accounts the Baroness was very haughty; and very whimsical.

COTTAGER. Wife, wife, never speak ill of the dead. Say what you please against the living, but not a word against the dead.

WIFE. And yet, husband, I believe the dead care the least what is said against them—And so, if you please, I'll tell my story. The late Baroness was, they say, haughty and proud; and they do say, the Baron was not so happy as he might have been; but he, bless him, our good Baron is still the same as when a boy. Soon after Madam had closed her eyes, he left France, and came to Waldenhaim, his native country.

COTTAGER. Many times has he joined in our village dances. Afterwards, when he became an officer, he was rather wild, as most young men are.

WIFE. Yes, I remember when he fell in love with poor Agatha, Friburg's daughter: what a piece of work that was—It did not do him much credit. That was a wicked thing.

COTTAGER. Have done—no more of this—It is not well to stir up old grievances.

WIFE. Why, you said I might speak ill of the living. 'Tis very hard indeed, if one must not speak ill of one's neighbours, dead, nor alive.

COTTAGER. Who knows whether he was the father of Agatha's child? She never said he was.

WIFE. Nobody but him—that I am sure—I would lay a wager—no, no husband—you must not take his part—it was very wicked! Who knows what is now become of that poor creature? She has not been heard of this many a year. May be she is starving for hunger. Her father might have lived longer too, if that misfortune had not happened.

[Agatha faints.]

COTTAGER. See here! Help! She is fainting—take hold!

WIFE. Oh, poor woman!

COTTAGER. Let us take her into the next room.

WIFE. Oh poor woman! —I am afraid she will not live. Come, chear up, chear up. —You are with those who feel for you. [They lead her off.]

SCENE II. An apartment in the Castle.

A table spread for breakfast—Several servants in livery disposing the equipage—BARON WILDENHAIM enters, attended by a GENTLEMAN in waiting.

BARON. Has not Count Cassel left his chamber yet?

GENTLEMAN. No, my lord, he has but now rung for his valet.

BARON. The whole castle smells of his perfumery. Go, call my daughter hither. [Exit Gentleman.] And am I after all to have an ape for a son-in-law? No, I shall not be in a hurry—I love my daughter too well. We must be better acquainted before I give her to him. I shall not sacrifice my Amelia to the will of others, as I myself was sacrificed. The poor girl might, in thoughtlessness, say yes, and afterwards be miserable. What a pity she is not a boy! The name of Wildenhaim will die with me. My fine estates, my good peasants, all will fall into the hands of strangers. Oh! why was not my Amelia a boy?

Enter AMELIA—[She kisses the Baron's hand.]

AMELIA. Good morning, dear my lord.

BARON. Good morning, Amelia. Have you slept well?

AMELIA. Oh! yes, papa. I always sleep well.

BARON. Not a little restless last night?

AMELIA. No.

BARON. Amelia, you know you have a father who loves you, and I believe you know you have a suitor who is come to ask permission to love you. Tell me candidly how you like Count Cassel?

AMELIA. Very well.

BARON. Do not you blush when I talk of him?

AMELIA. No.

BARON. No—I am sorry for that. aside] Have you dreamt of him?

AMELIA. No.

BARON. Have you not dreamt at all to-night?

AMELIA. Oh yes—I have dreamt of our chaplain, Mr. Anhalt.

BARON. Ah ha! As if he stood before you and the Count to ask for the ring.

AMELIA. No: not that—I dreamt we were all still in France, and he, my tutor, just going to take his leave of us for ever—I 'woke with the fright, and found my eyes full of tears.

BARON. Psha! I want to know if you can love the Count. You saw him at the last ball we were at in France: when he capered round you; when he danced minuets; when he——. But I cannot say what his conversation was.

AMELIA. Nor I either—I do not remember a syllable of it.

BARON. No? Then I do not think you like him.

AMELIA. I believe not.

BARON. But I think it proper to acquaint you he is rich, and of great consequence: rich and of consequence; do you hear?

AMELIA. Yes, dear papa. But my tutor has always told me that birth and fortune are inconsiderable things, and cannot give happiness.

BARON. There he is right—But of it happens that birth and fortune are joined with sense and virtue — —

AMELIA. But is it so with Count Cassel?

BARON. Hem! Hem! Aside.] I will ask you a few questions on this subject; but be sure to answer me honestly—Speak truth.

AMELIA. I never told an untruth in my life.

BARON. Nor ever *conceal* the truth from me, I command you.

AMELIA. [Earnestly.] Indeed, my lord, I never will.

BARON. I take you at your word—And now reply to me truly—Do you like to hear the Count spoken of?

AMELIA. Good, or bad?

BARON. Good. Good.

AMELIA. Oh yes; I like to here good of every body.

BARON. But do not you feel a little fluttered when he is talked of?

AMELIA. No. [shaking her head.]

BARON. Are not you a little embarrassed?

AMELIA. No.

BARON. Don't you wish sometimes to speak to him, and have not the courage to begin?

AMELIA. No.

BARON. Do not you wish to take his part when his companions laugh at him?

AMELIA. No—I love to laugh at him myself.

BARON. Provoking! Aside.] Are not you afraid of him when he comes near you?

AMELIA. No, not at all. —Oh yes—once. [recollecting herself.]

BARON. Ah! Now it comes!

AMELIA. Once at a ball he trod on my foot; and I was so afraid he should tread on me again.

BARON. You put me out of patience. Hear, Amelia! [stops short, and speaks softer. To see you happy is my wish. But matrimony, without concord, is like a duetto badly performed; for that reason, nature, the great composer of all harmony, has ordained, that, when bodies are allied, hearts should be in perfect unison. However, I will send Mr. Anhalt to you — —

AMELIA [much pleased]. Do, papa.

BARON. —He shall explain to you my sentiments. [Rings.] A clergyman can do this better than— —[Enter servant.] Go directly to Mr. Anhalt, tell him that I shall be glad to see him for a quarter of an hour if he is not engaged. [Exit servant.

AMELIA [calls after him]. Wish him a good morning from me.

BARON [looking at his watch]. The Count is a tedious time dressing. —Have you breakfasted, Amelia?

AMELIA. No, papa. [they sit down to breakfast.]

BARON. How is the weather? Have you walked this morning?

AMELIA. Oh, yes—I was in the garden at five o'clock; it is very fine.

BARON. Then I'll go out shooting. I do not know in what other way to amuse my guest.

Enter Count CASSEL.

COUNT. Ah, my dear Colonel! Miss Wildenhaim, I kiss your hand.

BARON. Good morning! Good morning! though it is late in the day, Count. In the country we should rise earlier.

[Amelia offers the Count a Cup of tea.]

COUNT. Is it Hebe herself, or Venus, or — —

AMELIA. Ha, ha, ha! Who can help laughing at his nonsense?

BARON [rather angry]. Neither Venus, nor Hebe; but Amelia Wildenhaim, if you please.

COUNT [Sitting down to breakfast]. You are beautiful, Miss Wildenhaim. —Upon my honour, I think so. I have travelled, and seen much of the world, and yet I can positively admire you.

18

COUNT. Wherefore?

AMELIA. Because I might then, perhaps, admire you.

COUNT. True; —for I am an epitome of the world. In my travels I learnt delicacy in Italy—hauteur, in Spain—in France, enterprize—in Russia, prudence—in England, sincerity—in Scotland, frugality—and in the wilds of America, I learnt love.

AMELIA. Is there any country where love is taught?

COUNT. In all barbarous countries. But the whole system is exploded in places that are civilized.

AMELIA. And what is substituted in its stead?

COUNT. Intrigue.

AMELIA. What a poor, uncomfortable substitute!

COUNT. There are other things—Song, dance, the opera, and war.

> [Since the entrance of the Count the Baron has removed to a table at a little distance.

BARON. What are you talking of there?

COUNT. Of war, Colonel.

BARON [rising]. Ay, we like to talk on what we don't understand.

COUNT [rising]. Therefore, to a lady, I always speak of politics; and to her father, on love.

BARON. I believe, Count, notwithstanding your sneer, I am still as much a proficient in that art as yourself.

COUNT. I do not doubt it, my dear Colonel, for you are a soldier: and since the days of Alexander, whoever conquers men is certain to overcome women.

BARON. An achievement to animate a poltroon.

COUNT. And, I verily believe, gains more recruits than the king's pay.

BARON. Now we are on the subject of arms, should you like to go out a shooting with me for an hour before dinner?

COUNT. Bravo, Colonel! A charming thought! This will give me an opportunity to use my elegant gun: the but is inlaid with mother-of-pearl. You cannot find better work, or better taste. —Even my coat of arms is engraved.

BARON. But can you shoot?

COUNT. That I have never tried—except, with my eyes, at a fine woman.

BARON. I am not particular what game I pursue. —I have an old gun; it does not look fine; But I can always bring down my bird.

> Enter SERVANT.

SERVANT. Mr. Anhalt begs leave— —

BARON. Tell him to come in. —I shall be ready in a moment. [Exit Servant.

COUNT. Who is Mr. Anhalt?

AMELIA. Oh, a very good man. [With warmth.]

COUNT. "A good man. " In Italy, that means a religious man; in France, it means a cheerful man; in Spain, it means a wise man; and in England, it means a rich man. —Which good of all these is Mr. Anhalt?

AMELIA. A good man in every country, except England.

COUNT. And give me the English good man, before that of any other nation.

BARON. And of what nation would you prefer your good woman to be, Count?

COUNT. Of Germany. [bowing to Amelia.]

AMELIA. In compliment to me?

COUNT. In justice to my own judgment.

BARON. Certainly. For have we not an instance of one German woman, who possesses every virtue that ornaments the whole sex; whether as a woman of illustrious rank, or in the more exalted character of a wife, and mother?

Enter Mr. ANHALT.

ANHALT. I come by your command, Baron — —

BARON. Quick, Count. —Get your elegant gun. —I pass your apartments, and will soon call for you.

COUNT. I fly. —Beautiful Amelia, it is a sacrifice I make to your father, that I leave for a few hours his amiable daughter. [Exit.]

BARON. My dear Amelia, I think it scarcely necessary to speak to Mr. Anhalt, or that he should speak to you, on the subject of the Count; but as he is here, leave us alone.

AMELIA [as she retires]. Good morning, Mr. Anhalt. —I hope you are very well. [Exit.]

BARON. I'll tell you in a few words why I sent for you. Count Cassel is here, and wishes to marry my daughter.

ANHALT [much concerned]. Really!

BARON. He is—he—in a word I don't like him.

ANHALT [with emotion]. And Miss Wildenhaim — —

BARON. I shall not command, neither persuade her to the marriage—I know too well the fatal influence of parents on such a subject. Objections to be sure, if they could be removed—But when you find a man's head without brains, and his bosom without a heart, these are important articles to supply. Young as you are, Anhalt, I know no one so able to restore, or to bestow those blessings

21

on his fellow-creatures, as you. [Anhalt bows.] The Count wants a little of my daughter's simplicity and sensibility. —Take him under your care while he is here, and make him something like yourself. — You have succeeded to my wish in the education of my daughter. — Form the Count after your own manner. —I shall then have what I have sighed for all my life—a son.

ANHALT. With your permission, Baron, I will ask one question. What remains to interest you in favour of a man, whose head and heart are good for nothing?

BARON. Birth and fortune. Yet, if I thought my daughter absolutely disliked him, or that she loved another, I would not thwart a first affection; — no, for the world, I would not. [sighing.] But that her affections are already bestowed, is not probable.

ANHALT. Are you of opinion that she will never fall in love?

BARON. Oh! no. I am of opinion that no woman ever arrived at the age of twenty without that misfortune. —But this is another subject. —Go to Amelia—explain to her the duties of a wife and of a mother. —If she comprehends them, as she ought, then ask her if she thinks she could fulfil those duties, as the wife of Count Cassel.

ANHALT. I will. —But—I—Miss Wildenhaim—[confused. I—I shall—I—I shall obey your commands.

BARON. Do so. [gives a deep sigh. Ah! so far this weight is removed; but there lies still a heavier next my heart. —You understand me. — How is it, Mr. Anhalt? Have you not yet been able to make any discoveries on that unfortunate subject?

ANHALT. I have taken infinite pains; but in vain. No such person is to be found.

BARON. Believe me, this burthen presses on my thoughts so much, that many nights I go without sleep. A man is sometimes tempted to commit such depravity when young. —Oh, Anhalt! had I, in my youth, had you for a tutor; —but I had no instructor but my passions; no governor but my own will. [Exit.

ANHALT. This commission of the Baron's in respect to his daughter, I am—[looks about]—If I shou'd meet her now, I cannot—I must recover myself first, and then prepare. —A walk in the fields, and a fervent prayer—After these, I trust, I shall return, as a man whose views are solely placed on a future world; all hopes in this, with fortitude resigned. [Exit.

END ACT II.

ACT III.

SCENE I. An open Field.

FREDERICK alone, with a few pieces of money which he turns about in his hands.

FREDERICK. To return with this trifle for which I have stooped to beg! return to see my mother dying! I would rather fly to the world's end. [Looking at the money.] What can I buy with this? It is hardly enough to pay for the nails that will be wanted for her coffin. My great anxiety will drive me to distraction. However, let the consequence of our affliction be what it may, all will fall upon my father's head; and may he pant for Heaven's forgiveness, as my poor mother — — [At a distance is heard the firing of a gun, then the cry of Hallo, Hallo—Gamekeepers and Sportsmen run across the stage— he looks about.] Here they come—a nobleman, I suppose, or a man of fortune. Yes, yes—and I will once more beg for my mother. —May Heaven send relief!

> Enter the BARON followed slowly by the COUNT. The BARON stops.

BARON. Quick, quick, Count! Aye, aye, that was a blunder indeed. Don't you see the dogs? There they run—they have lost the scent. [Exit Baron looking after the dogs.

COUNT. So much the better, Colonel, for I must take a little breath. [He leans on his gun—Frederick goes up to him with great modesty.]

FREDERICK. Gentleman, I beg you will bestow from your superfluous wants something to relieve the pain, and nourish the weak frame, of an expiring woman.

> The BARON re-enters.

COUNT. What police is here! that a nobleman's amusements should be interrupted by the attack of vagrants.

FREDERICK [to the Baron]. Have pity, noble Sir, and relieve the distress of an unfortunate son, who supplicates for his dying mother.

24

BARON [taking out his purse]. I think, young soldier, it would be better if you were with your regiment on duty, instead of begging.

FREDERICK. I would with all my heart: but at this present moment my sorrows are too great. —[Baron gives something.] I entreat your pardon. What you have been so good as to give me is not enough.

BARON [surprised]. Not enough!

FREDERICK. No, it is not enough.

COUNT. The most singular beggar I ever met in all my travels.

FREDERICK. If you have a charitable heart, give me one dollar.

BARON. This is the first time I was ever dictated by a beggar what to give him.

FREDERICK. With one dollar you will save a distracted man.

BARON. I don't choose to give any more. Count, go on.

> [Exit Count—as the Baron follows, Frederick seizes him by the breast and draws his sword.]

FREDERICK. Your purse, or your life.

BARON [calling]. Here! here! seize and secure him.

> [Some of the Gamekeepers run on, lay hold of Frederick, and disarm him.]

FREDERICK. What have I done!

BARON. Rake him to the castle, and confine him in one of the towers. I shall follow you immediately.

FREDERICK. One favour I have to beg, one favour only. —I know that I am guilty, and am ready to receive the punishment my crime deserves. But I have a mother, who is expiring for want—pity her, if you cannot pity me—bestow on her relief. If you will send to yonder hut, you will find that I do not impose on you a falsehood. For her it was I drew my sword—for her I am ready to die.

BARON. Take him away, and imprison him where I told you.

FREDERICK [as he is forced off by the keepers]. Woe to that man to whom I owe my birth! [Exit.

BARON [calls another Keeper]. Here, Frank, run directly to yonder hamlet, inquire in the first, second, and third cottage for a poor sick woman—and if you really find such a person, give her this purse. [Exit Gamekeeper.]

BARON. A most extraordinary event! —and what a well-looking youth! something in his countenance and address which struck me inconceivably! —If it is true that he begged for his mother—But if he did——for the attempt upon my life, he must die. Vice is never half so dangerous, as when it assumes the garb of morality. [Exit.]

SCENE II. A room in the Castle.

AMELIA [alone.] Why am I so uneasy; so peevish; who has offended me? I did not mean to come into this room. In the garden I intended to go [going, turns back]. No, I will not—yes, I will—just go, and look if my auriculas are still in blossom; and if the apple tree is grown which Mr. Anhalt planted. —I feel very low-spirited— something must be the matter. —Why do I cry? —Am I not well?

Enter Mr. ANHALT.

Ah! good morning, my dear Sir—Mr. Anhalt, I meant to say—I beg pardon.

ANHALT. Never mind, Miss Wildenhaim—I don't dislike to hear you call me as you did.

AMELIA. In earnest?

ANHALT. Really. You have been crying. May I know the reason? The loss of your mother, still? —

AMELIA. No—I have left off crying for her.

ANHALT. I beg pardon if I have come at an improper hour; but I wait upon you by the commands of your father.

AMELIA. You are welcome at all hours. My father has more than once told me that he who forms my mind I should always consider as my greatest benefactor. [looking down] And my heart tells me the same.

ANHALT. I think myself amply rewarded by the good opinion you have of me.

AMELIA. When I remember what trouble I have sometimes given you, I cannot be too grateful.

ANHALT [to himself]. Oh! Heavens! —[to Amelia]. I—I come from your father with a commission. —If you please, we will sit down. [He places chairs, and they sit.] Count Cassel is arrived.

AMELIA. Yes, I know.

ANHALT. And do you know for what reason?

AMELIA. He wishes to marry me.

ANHALT. Does he? hastily] But believe me, the Baron will not persuade you—No, I am sure he will not.

AMELIA. I know that.

ANHALT. He wishes that I should ascertain whether you have an inclination — —

AMELIA. For the Count, or for matrimony do you mean?

ANHALT. For matrimony.

AMELIA. All things that I don't know, and don't understand, are quite indifferent to me.

ANHALT. For that very reason I am sent to you to explain the good and the bad of which matrimony is composed.

AMELIA. Then I beg first to be acquainted with the good.

ANHALT. When two sympathetic hearts meet in the marriage state, matrimony may be called a happy life. When such a wedded pair find thorns in their path, each will be eager, for the sake of the other, to tear them from the root. Where they have to mount hills, or wind a labyrinth, the most experienced will lead the way, and be a guide to his companion. Patience and love will accompany them in their journey, while melancholy and discord they leave far behind. — Hand in hand they pass on from morning till evening, through their summer's day, till the night of age draws on, and the sleep of death overtakes the one. The other, weeping and mourning, yet looks forward to the bright region where he shall meet his still surviving partner, among trees and flowers which themselves have planted, in fields of eternal verdure.

AMELIA. You may tell my father—I'll marry. [Rises.]

ANHALT [rising]. This picture is pleasing; but I must beg you not to forget that there is another on the same subject. —When convenience, and fair appearance joined to folly and ill-humour, forge the fetters of matrimony, they gall with their weight the married pair. Discontented with each other—at variance in opinions—their mutual aversion increases with the years they live together. They contend most, where they should most unite; torment, where they should most soothe. In this rugged way, choaked with the weeds of suspicion, jealousy, anger, and hatred, they take their daily journey, till one of these *also* sleep in death. The other then lifts up his dejected head, and calls out in acclamations of joy—Oh, liberty! dear liberty!

AMELIA. I will not marry.

ANHALT. You mean to say, you will not fall in love.

AMELIA. Oh no! [ashamed] I am in love.

ANHALT. Are in love! [starting] And with the Count?

AMELIA. I wish I was.

ANHALT. Why so?

AMELIA. Because *he* would, perhaps, love me again.

ANHALT [warmly]. Who is there that would not?

AMELIA. Would you?

ANHALT. I—I—me—I—I am out of the question.

AMELIA. No; you are the very person to whom I have put the question.

ANHALT. What do you mean?

AMELIA. I am glad you don't understand me. I was afraid I had spoken too plain. [in confusion].

ANHALT. Understand you! —As to that—I am not dull.

29

AMELIA. I know you are not—And as you have for a long time instructed me, why should not I now begin to teach you?

ANHALT. Teach me what?

AMELIA. Whatever I know, and you don't.

ANHALT. There are some things I had rather never know.

AMELIA. So you may remember I said when You began to teach me mathematics. I said I had rather not know it—But now I have learnt it gives me a great deal of pleasure—and [hesitating] perhaps, who can tell, but that I might teach something as pleasant to you, as resolving a problem is to me.

ANHALT. Woman herself is a problem.

AMELIA. And I'll teach you to make her out.

ANHALT. *You* teach?

AMELIA. Why not? none but a woman can teach the science of herself: and though I own I am very young, a young woman may be as agreeable for a tutoress as an old one. —I am sure I always learnt faster from you than from the old clergyman who taught me before you came.

ANHALT. This is nothing to the subject.

AMELIA. What is the subject?

ANHALT. — — Love.

AMELIA [going up to him]. Come, then, teach it me—teach it me as you taught me geography, languages, and other important things

ANHALT [turning from her] Pshaw!

AMELIA. Ah! you won't—You know you have already taught me that, and you won't begin again.

ANHALT. You misconstrue—you misconceive every thing I say or do. The subject I came to you upon was marriage.

AMELIA. A very proper subject from the man who has taught me love, and I accept the proposal [curtsying].

ANHALT. Again you misconceive and confound me.

AMELIA. Ay, I see how it is—You have no inclination to experience with me "the good part of matrimony: " I am not the female with whom you would like to go "hand in hand up hills, and through labyrinths"—with whom you would like to "root up thorns; and with whom you would delight to plant lilies and roses. " No, you had rather call out, "O liberty, dear liberty. "

ANHALT. Why do you force from me, what it is villanous to own? —I love you more than life—Oh, Amelia! had we lived in those golden times, which the poet's picture, no one but you — — But as the world is changed, your birth and fortune make our union impossible—To preserve the character, and more the feelings of an honest man, I would not marry you without the consent of your father—And could I, dare I propose it to him.

AMELIA. He has commanded me never to conceal or disguise the truth. I will propose it to him. The subject of the Count will force me to speak plainly, and this will be the most proper time, while he can compare the merit of you both.

ANHALT. I conjure you not to think of exposing yourself and me to his resentment.

AMELIA. It is my father's will that I should marry—It is my father's wish to see me happy—If then you love me as you say, I will marry; and will be happy—but only with you. —I will tell him this. —At first he will start; then grow angry; then be in a passion—In his passion he will call me "undutiful: " but he will soon recollect himself, and resume his usual smiles, saying "Well, well, if he love you, and you love him, in the name of heaven, let it be. "—Then I shall hug him round the neck, kiss his hands, run away from him, and fly to you; it will soon be known that I am your bride, the whole village will come to wish me joy, and heaven's blessing will follow.

Enter Verdun, the BUTLER.

AMELIA [discontented]. Ah! is it you?

31

BUTLER. Without vanity, I have taken the liberty to enter this apartment the moment the good news reached my ears.

AMELIA. What news?

BUTLER. Pardon an old servant, your father's old butler, gracious lady, who has had the honour to carry the baron in his arms—and afterwards with humble submission to receive many a box o' the ear from you—if he thinks it his duty to make his congratulations with due reverence on this happy day, and to join with the muses in harmonious tunes on the lyre.

AMELIA. Oh! my good butler, I am not in a humour to listen to the muses, and your lyre.

BUTLER. There has never been a birth-day, nor wedding-day, nor christening-day, celebrated in your family, in which I have not joined with the muses in full chorus. —In forty-six years, three hundred and ninety-seven congratulations on different occasions have dropped from my pen. To-day, the three hundred and ninety-eighth is coming forth; —for heaven has protected our noble master, who has been in great danger.

AMELIA. Danger! My father in danger! What do you mean?

BUTLER. One of the gamekeepers has returned to inform the whole castle of a base and knavish trick, of which the world will talk, and my poetry hand down to posterity.

AMELIA. What, what is all this.

BUTLER. The baron, my lord and master, in company with the strange Count, had not been gone a mile beyond the lawn, when one of them — —

AMELIA. What happened? Speak for heaven's sake.

BUTLER. My verse shall tell you.

AMELIA. No, no; tell us in prose.

ANHALT. Yes, in prose.

BUTLER. Ah, you have neither of you ever been in love, or you would prefer poetry to prose. But excuse [pulls out a paper] the haste in which it was written. I heard the news in the fields—always have paper and a pencil about me, and composed the whole forty lines crossing the meadows and the park in my way home. [reads.]

> Oh Muse, ascend the forked mount.
>   And lofty strains prepare,
> About a Baron and a Count,
>   Who went to hunt the hare.
>
> The hare she ran with utmost speed,
>   And sad, and anxious looks,
> Because the furious hounds indeed,
>   Were near to her, gadzooks.
>
> At length, the Count and Baron bold
>   Their footsteps homeward bended;
> For why, because, as you were told,
>   The hunting it was ended.
>
> Before them strait a youth appears,
>   Who made a piteous pother,
> And told a tale with many tears,
>   About his dying mother.
>
> The youth was in severe distress,
>   And seem'd as he had spent all,
> He look'd a soldier by his dress;
>   For that was regimental.
>
> The Baron's heart was full of ruth,
>   While from his eye fell brine o!
> And soon he gave the mournful youth
>   A little ready rino.
>
> He gave a shilling as I live,
>   Which, sure, was mighty well;
> But to some people if you give
>   An inch—they'll take an ell.
>
> The youth then drew his martial knife,
>   And seiz'd the Baron's collar,

He swore he'd have the Baron's life,
  Or else another dollar.

Then did the Baron in a fume,
  Soon raise a mighty din,
Whereon came butler, huntsman, groom,
  And eke the whipper-in.

Maugre this young man's warlike coat,
  They bore him off to prison;
And held so strongly by his throat,
  They almost stopt his whizzen.

Soon may a neckcloth, call'd a rope,
  Of robbing cure this elf;
If so I'll write, without a trope,
  His dying speech myself.

And had the Baron chanc'd to die,
  Oh! grief to all the nation,
I must have made an elegy,
  And not this fine narration.

MORAL.

Henceforth let those who all have spent,
  And would by begging live,
Take warning here, and be content,
  With what folks chuse to give.

AMELIA. Your muse, Mr. Butler, is in a very inventive humour this morning.

ANHALT. And your tale too improbable, even for fiction.

BUTLER. Improbable! It's a real fact.

AMELIA. What, a robber in our grounds, at noon-day? Very likely indeed!

BUTLER. I don't say it was likely—I only say it is true.

ANHALT. No, no, Mr. Verdun, we find no fault with your poetry; but don't attempt to impose it upon us for truth.

AMELIA. Poets are allowed to speak falsehood, and we forgive yours.

BUTLER. I won't be forgiven, for I speak truth—And here the robber comes, in custody, to prove my words. [Goes off, repeating] "I'll write his dying speech myself. "

AMELIA. Look! as I live, so he does—They come nearer; he's a young man, and has something interesting in his figure. An honest countenance, with grief and sorrow in his face. No, he is no robber—I pity him! Oh! look how the keepers drag him unmercifully into the tower—Now they lock it—Oh! how that poor, unfortunate man must feel!

ANHALT [aside]. Hardly worse than I do.

Enter the BARON.

AMELIA [runs up to him]. A thousand congratulations, my dear papa.

BARON. For Heaven's sake spare me your congratulations. The old Butler, in coming up stairs, has already overwhelmed me with them.

ANHALT. Then, it is true, my Lord? I could hardly believe the old man.

AMELIA. And the young prisoner, with all his honest looks, is a robber?

BARON. He is; but I verily believe for the first and last time. A most extraordinary event, Mr. Anhalt This young man begged; then drew his sword upon me; but he trembled so, when he seized me by the breast, a child might have overpowered him. I almost wish he had made his escape—this adventure may cost him his life, and I might have preserved it with one dollar: but, now, to save him would set a bad example.

AMELIA. Oh no! my lord, have pity on him! Plead for him, Mr. Anhalt!

Lover's Vows

BARON. Amelia, have you had any conversation with Mr. Anhalt?

AMELIA. Yes, my Lord.

BARON. Respecting matrimony?

AMELIA. Yes; and I have told him — —

ANHALT [very hastily]. According to your commands, Baron — —

AMELIA. But he has conjured me — —

ANHALT. I have endeavoured, my Lord, to find out — —

AMELIA. Yet, I am sure, dear papa, your affection for me — —

ANHALT. You wish to say something to me in your closet, my Lord?

BARON. What the devil is all this conversation? You will not let one another speak—I don't understand either of you.

AMELIA. Dear father, have you not promised you will not thwart my affections when I marry, but suffer me to follow their dictates.

BARON. Certainly.

AMELIA. Do you hear, Mr. Anhalt?

ANHALT. I beg pardon—I have a person who is waiting for me—I am obliged to retire. [Exit in confusion.

BARON [calls after him]. I shall expect you in my closet. I am going there immediately. [Retiring towards the opposite door.]

AMELIA. Pray, my Lord, stop a few minutes longer; I have something of great importance to say to you.

BARON. Something of importance! to plead for the young man, I suppose! But that's a subject I must not listen to. [Exit.

AMELIA. I wish to plead for two young men—For one, that he may be let out of prison: for the other, that he may be made a prisoner for life. [Looks out.] The tower is still locked. How dismal it must be to be shut up in such a place; and perhaps—[Calls] Butler! Butler! Come this way. I wish to speak to you. This young soldier has risked his life for his mother, and that accounts for the interest I take in his misfortunes.

Enter the BUTLER.

Pray, have you carried anything to the prisoner to eat?

BUTLER. Yes.

AMELIA. What was it?

BUTLER. Some fine black bread; and water as clear as crystal.

AMELIA. Are you not ashamed! Even my father pities him. Go directly down to the kitchen, and desire the cook to give you something good and comfortable; and then go into the cellar for a bottle of wine.

BUTLER. Good and comfortable indeed!

AMELIA. And carry both to the tower.

BUTLER. I am willing at any time, dear Lady, to obey your orders; but, on this occasion, the prisoner's food must remain bread and water—It is the Baron's particular command.

AMELIA. Ah! My father was in the height of passion when he gave it.

BUTLER. Whatsoever his passion might be, it is the duty of a true, and honest dependent to obey his Lord's mandates. I will not suffer a servant in this house, nor will I, myself, give the young man any thing except bread and water—But I'll tell you what I'll do—I'll read my verses to him.

AMELIA. Give me the key of the cellar—I'll go myself.

BUTLER [gives the key]. And there's my verses—[taking them from his pocket] Carry them with you, they may comfort him as much as the wine. [She throws them down. [Exit Amelia.

BUTLER [in amazement]. Not take them! Refuse to take them—[he lifts them from the floor with the utmost respect]—

"I must have made an elegy,
And not this fine narration. " [Exit.

END ACT III

ACT IV.

FREDERICK. How a few moments destroy the happiness of man! When I, this morning, set out from my inn, and saw the sun rise, I sung with joy. —Flattered with the hope of seeing my mother, I formed a scheme how I would with joy surprize her. But, farewell all pleasant prospects—I return to my native country, and the first object I behold, is my dying parent; my first lodging, a prison; and my next walk will perhaps be—oh, merciful providence! have I deserved all this?

> Enter AMELIA with a small basket covered with a napkin. —She speaks to someone without.

AMELIA. Wait there, Francis, I shall soon be back.

FREDERICK [hearing the door open, and turning around]. Who's there?

AMELIA. You must be hungry and thirsty, I fear.

FREDERICK. Oh, no! neither.

AMELIA. Here is a bottle of wine, and something to eat. [Places the basket on the table.] I have often heard my father say, that wine is quite a cordial to the heart.

FREDERICK. A thousand thanks, dear stranger. Ah! could I prevail on you to have it sent to my mother, who is on her death-bed, under the roof of an honest peasant, called Hubert! Take it hence, my kind benefactress, and save my mother.

AMELIA. But first assure me that you did not intend to murder my father.

FREDERICK. Your father! heaven forbid. —I meant but to preserve her life, who gave me mine. —Murder your father! No, no—I hope not.

AMELIA. And I thought not—Or, if you had murdered any one, you had better have killed the Count; nobody would have missed him.

FREDERICK. Who, may I enquire, were those gentlemen, whom I hoped to frighten into charity?

AMELIA. Ay, if you only intended to frighten them, the Count was the very person for your purpose. But you caught hold of the other gentleman. —And could you hope to intimidate Baron Wildenhaim?

FREDERICK. Baron Wildenhaim! —Almighty powers!

AMELIA. What's the matter?

FREDERICK. The man to whose breast I held my sword— [trembling].

AMELIA. Was Baron Wildenhaim—the owner of this estate—my father!

FREDERICK [with the greatest emotion]. *My* father!

AMELIA. Good heaven, how he looks! I am afraid he's mad. Here! Francis, Francis. [Exit, calling.

FREDERICK [all agitation]. My *father*! Eternal judge! tho do'st slumber! The man, against whom I drew my sword this day was my father! One moment longer, and provoked, I might have been the murderer of my father! my hair stands on end! my eyes are clouded! I cannot see any thing before me. [Sinks down on chair]. If Providence had ordained that I should give the fatal blow, who, would have been most in fault? —I dare not pronounce— after a pause] That benevolent young female who left me just now, is, then, my sister—and I suppose that fop, who accompanied my father—

Enter Mr. ANHALT.

Welcome, Sir! By your dress you are of the church, and consequently a messenger of comfort. You are most welcome, Sir.

ANHALT. I wish to bring comfort and avoid upbraidings: for your own conscience will reproach you more than the voice of a preacher. From the sensibility of your countenance, together with a language, and address superior to the vulgar, it appears, young man, you have had an education, which should have preserved you from a state like this.

FREDERICK. My education I owe to my mother. Filial love, in return, has plunged me into the state you see. A civil magistrate will condemn according to the law—A priest, in judgment, is not to consider the act itself, but the impulse which led to the act.

ANHALT. I shall judge with all the lenity my religion dictates: and you are the prisoner of a nobleman, who compassionates you for the affection which you bear towards your mother; for he has sent to the village where you directed him, and has found the account you gave relating to her true. —With this impression in your favour, it is my advice, that you endeavour to see and supplicate the Baron for your release from prison, and all the peril of his justice.

FREDERICK [starting]. I—I see the Baron! I! —I supplicate for my deliverance. —Will you favour me with his name? —Is it not Baron— —

ANHALT. Baron Wildenhaim.

FREDERICK. Baron Wildenhaim! He lived formerly in Alsace.

ANHALT. The same. —About a year after the death of his wife, he left Alsace; and arrived here a few weeks ago to take possession of his paternal estate.

FREDERICK. So! his wife is dead; —and that generous young lady who came to my prison just now is his daughter?

ANHALT. Miss Wildenhaim, his daughter.

FREDERICK. And that young gentleman, I saw with him this morning, is his son?

ANHALT. He has no son.

FREDERICK [hastily]. Oh, yes, he has—[recollecting himself]—I mean him that was out shooting to-day.

ANHALT. He is not his son.

41

FREDERICK [to himself]. Thank Heaven!

ANHALT. He is only a visitor.

FREDERICK. I thank you for this information; and if you will undertake to procure me a private interview with Baron Wildenhaim— —

ANHALT. Why private? However, I will venture to take you for a short time from this place, and introduce you; depending on your innocence, or your repentance—on his conviction in your favour, or his mercy towards your guilt. Follow me. [Exit.

FREDERICK [following]. I have beheld an affectionate parent in deep adversity. —Why should I tremble thus? —Why doubt my fortitude, in the presence of an unnatural parent in prosperity? [Exit.

Lover's Vows

SCENE II. A Room in the Castle.

Enter BARON WILDENHAIM and AMELIA.

BARON. I hope you will judge more favourably of Count Cassel's understanding since the private interview you have had with him. Confess to me the exact effect of the long conference between you.

AMELIA. To make me hate him.

BARON. What has he done?

AMELIA. Oh! told me of such barbarous deeds he has committed.

BARON. What deeds?

AMELIA. Made vows of love to so many women, that, on his marriage with me, a hundred female hearts will at least be broken.

BARON. Psha! do you believe him?

AMELIA. Suppose I do not; is it to his honour that I believe he tells a falsehood?

BARON. He is mistaken merely.

AMELIA. Indeed, my Lord, in one respect I am sure he speaks truth. For our old Butler told my waiting-maid of a poor young creature who has been deceived, undone; and she, and her whole family, involved in shame and sorrow by his perfidy.

BARON. Are you sure the Butler said this?

AMELIA. See him and ask him. He knows the whole of story, indeed he does; the names of the persons, and every circumstance.

BARON. Desire he may be sent to me.

AMELIA [goes to the door and calls]. Order old Verdun to come to the Baron directly.

BARON. I know tale-bearers are apt to be erroneous. I'll hear from himself, the account you speak of.

AMELIA. I believe it is in verse.

BARON. [angry]. In verse!

AMELIA. But, then, indeed it's true.

Enter BUTLER.

AMELIA. Verdun, pray have not you some true poetry?

BUTLER. All my poetry is true—and so far, better than some people's prose.

BARON. But I want prose on this occasion, and command you to give me nothing else. [Butler bows.] Have you heard of an engagement which Count Cassel is under to any other woman than my daughter?

BUTLER. I am to tell your honour in prose?

BARON. Certainly. [Butler appears uneasy and loath to speak.] Amelia, he does not like to divulge what he knows in presence of a third person—leave the room. [Exit Amelia.

BUTLER. No, no—that did not cause my reluctance to speak.

BARON. What then?

BUTLER. Your not allowing me to speak in verse—for here is the poetic poem. [Holding up a paper.]

BARON. How dare you presume to contend with my will? Tell in plain language all you know on the subject I have named.

BUTLER. Well, then, my Lord, if you must have the account in quiet prose, thus it was—Phoebus, one morning, rose in the East, and having handed in the long-expected day, he called up his brother Hymen——

BARON. Have done with your rhapsody.

BUTLER. Ay; I knew you'd like it best in verse— —

> There lived a lady in this land,
> Whose charms the heart made tingle;
> At church she had not given her hand,
> And therefore still was single.

BARON. Keep to prose.

BUTLER. I will, mu Lord; but I have repeated it so often in verse, I scarce know how. —Count Cassel, influenced by the designs of Cupid in his very worst humour,

> "Count Cassel wooed this maid so rare,
> And in her eye found grace;
> And if his purpose was not fair,"

BARON. No verse.

BUTLER.
> "It probably was base."

I beg pardon, my Lord; but the verse will intrude in spite of my efforts to forget it. 'Tis as difficult for me at times to forget, as 'tis for other men at times to remember. But in plain truth, my Lord, the Count was treacherous, cruel, forsworn.

BARON. I am astonished!

BUTLER. And would be more so if you would listen to the whole poem. [Most earnestly.] Pray, my Lord, listen to it.

BARON. You know the family? All the parties?

BUTLER. I will bring the father of the damsel to prove the veracity of my muse. His name is Baden—poor old man!

> "The sire consents to bless the pair,
> And names the nuptial day,
> When, lo! the bridegroom was not there,
> Because he was away."

BARON. But tell me—Had the father his daughter's innocence to deplore?

BUTLER. Ah! my Lord, ah! and you *must* hear that part in rhyme. Loss of innocence never sounds well except in verse.

"For ah! the very night before,
No prudent guard upon her,
The Count he gave her oaths a score,
And took in change her honour.

MORAL.
Then you, who now lead single lives,
From this sad tale beware;
And do not act as you were wives,
Before you really are."

Enter COUNT CASSEL.

BARON [to the Butler]. Leave the room instantly.

COUNT. Yes, good Mr. family poet, leave the room, and take your doggerels with you.

BUTLER. Don't affront my poem, your honour; for I am indebted to you for the plot.

"The Count he gave her oaths a score
And took in change her honour."
[Exit Butler.

BARON. Count, you see me agitated.

COUNT. What can be the cause?

BARON. I'll not keep you in doubt a moment. You are accused, young man, of being engaged to another woman while you offer marriage to my child.

COUNT. To only *one* other woman?

BARON. What do you mean?

COUNT. My meaning is, that when a man is young and rich, has travelled, and is no personal object of disapprobation, to have made vows but to one woman, is an absolute slight upon the rest of the sex.

BARON. Without evasion, Sir, do you know the name of Baden? Was there ever a promise of marriage made by you to his daughter? Answer me plainly: or must I take a journey to inquire of the father?

COUNT. No—he can tell you no more than, I dare say, you already know; and which I shall not contradict.

BARON. Amazing insensibility! And can you hold your head erect while you acknowledge perfidy?

COUNT. My dear baron, —if every man, who deserves to have a charge such as this brought against him, was not permitted to look up—it is a doubt whom we might not meet crawling on all fours. [he accidently taps the Baron's shoulder.]

BARON [starts—recollects himself—then in a faultering voice]. Yet—nevertheless-the act is so atrocious—

COUNT. But nothing new.

BARON [faintly]. Yes—I hope—I hope it is new.

COUNT. What, did you never meet with such a thing before?

BARON [agitated]. If I have—I pronounced the man who so offended—a villain.

COUNT. You are singularly scrupulous. I question if the man thought himself so.

BARON. Yes he did.

COUNT. How do you know?

BARON [hesitating]. I have heard him say so.

COUNT. But he ate, drank, and slept, I suppose?

BARON [confused]. Perhaps he did.

COUNT. And was merry with his friends; and his friends as fond of him as ever?

BARON. Perhaps [confused]—perhaps they were.

COUNT. And perhaps he now and then took upon him to lecture young men for their gallantries?

BARON. Perhaps he did.

COUNT. Why, then, after all, Baron, your villain is a mighty good, prudent, honest fellow; and I have no objection to your giving me that name.

BARON. But do you not think of some atonement to the unfortunate girl?

COUNT. Did *your* villain atone?

BARON. No: when his reason was matured, he wished to make some recompense; but his endeavours were too late.

COUNT. I will follow his example, and wait till my reason is matured, before I think myself competent to determine what to do.

BARON. And 'till that time I defer your marriage with my daughter.

COUNT. Would you delay her happiness so long? Why, my dear Baron, considering the fashionable life I lead, it may be ten years before my judgment arrives to its necessary standard.

BARON. I have the head-ach, Count—These tidings have discomposed, disordered me—I beg your absence for a few minutes.

COUNT. I obey—And let me assure you, my Lord, that, although, from the extreme delicacy of your honour, you have ever through life shuddered at seduction; yet, there are constitutions, and there are circumstances, in which it can be palliated.

BARON. Never [violently].

COUNT. Not in a grave, serious, reflecting man such as *you*, I grant. But in a gay, lively, inconsiderate, flimsy, frivolous coxcomb, such as myself, it is excusable: for me to keep my word to a woman, would be deceit: 'tis not expected of me. It is in my character to break oaths in love; as it is in your nature, my Lord, never to have spoken any thing but wisdom and truth. [Exit

BARON. Could I have thought a creature so insignificant as that, had power to excite sensations such as I feel at present! I am, indeed, worse than he is, as much as the crimes of a man exceed those of an idiot.

Enter AMELIA.

AMELIA. I heard the Count leave you, my Lord, and so I am come to enquire——

BARON [sitting down, and trying to compose himself]. You are not to marry count Cassel—And now, mention his name to me no more.

AMELIA. I won't—indeed I won't—for I hate his name. —But thank you, my dear father, for this good news [draws a chair, and sits on the opposite side of the table on which he leans. —And after a pause] And who am I to marry?

BARON [his head on his hand]. I can't tell.

[Amelia appears to have something on her mind which she wishes to disclose.]

AMELIA. I never liked the Count.

BARON. No more did I.

AMELIA [after a pause]. I think love comes just as it pleases, without being asked.

BARON. It does so [in deep thought].

AMELIA [after another pause]. And there are instances where, perhaps, the object of love makes the passion meritorious.

BARON. To be sure there are.

AMELIA. For example; my affection for Mr. Anhalt as my tutor.

BARON. Right.

AMELIA [after another pause]. I should like to marry. [sighing.]

BARON. So you shall [a pause]. It is proper for every body to marry.

AMELIA. Why, then, does not Mr. Anhalt marry?

BARON. You must ask him that question yourself.

AMELIA. A have.

BARON. And what did he say?

AMELIA. Will you give me leave to tell you what he said?

BARON. Certainly.

AMELIA. And you won't be angry?

BARON. Undoubtedly not.

AMELIA. Why, then—you know you commanded me never to disguise or conceal the truth.

BARON. I did so.

AMELIA. Why, then he said — —

BARON. What did he say?

AMELIA. He said—he would not marry me without your consent for the world.

BARON [starting from his chair]. And pray, how came this the subject of your conversation?

AMELIA [rising]. *I* brought it up.

BARON. And what did you say?

AMELIA. I said that birth and fortune were such old-fashioned things to me, I cared nothing about either: and that I had once heard my father declare, he should consult my happiness in marrying me, beyond any other consideration.

BARON. I will once more repeat to you my sentiments. It is the custom in this country for the children of nobility to marry only with their equals; but as my daughter's content is more dear to me than an ancient custom, I would bestow you on the first man I thought calculated to make you happy: by this I do not mean to say that I should not be severely nice in the character of the man to whom I gave you; and Mr. Anhalt, from his obligations to me, and his high sense of honour, thinks too nobly—

AMELIA. Would it not be noble to make the daughter of his benefactor happy?

BARON. But when that daughter is a child, and thinks like a child——

AMELIA. No, indeed, papa, I begin to think very like a woman. Ask *him* if I don't.

BARON. Ask him! You feel gratitude for the instructions you have received from him, and fancy it love.

AMELIA. Are there two gratitudes?

BARON. What do you mean?

AMELIA. Because I feel gratitude to you; but that os very unlike the gratitude I feel towards him.

BARON. Indeed!

AMELIA. Yes; and then he feels another gratitude towards me. What's that?

BARON. Has he told you so?

AMELIA. Yes.

BARON. That was not right of him.
AMELIA. Oh! if you did but know how I surprised him!

Lover's Vows

BARON. Surprized him?

AMELIA. He came to me by your command, to examine my heart respecting Count Cassel. I told him that I would never marry the Count.

BARON. But him?

AMELIA. Yes, him.

BARON. Very fine indeed! And what was his answer?

AMELIA. He talked of my rank in life; of my aunts and cousins; of my grandfather, and great-grandfather; of his duty to you; and endeavoured to persuade me to think no more of him.

BARON. He acted honestly.

AMELIA. But not politely.

BARON. No matter.

AMELIA. Dear father! I shall never be able to love another—Never be happy with any one else. [Throwing herself on her knees.]

BARON. Rise, I command you.

[As she rises, enter ANHALT.]

ANHALT. My Lord, forgive me! I have ventured, on the privilege of my office, as a minister of holy charity, to bring the poor soldier, whom your justice has arrested, into the adjoining room; and I presume to entreat you will admit him to your presence, and hear his apology, or his supplication.

BARON. Anhalt, you have done wrong. I pity the unhappy boy; but you know I cannot, must not forgive him.

ANHALT. I beseech you then, my Lord, to tell him so yourself. From your lips he may receive his doom with resignation.

AMELIA. Oh father! See him and take pity on him; his sorrows have made him frantic.

BARON. Leave the room, Amelia. [on her attempting to speak, he raises his voice.] Instantly. —[Exit Amelia.

ANHALT. He asked for a private audience: perhaps he has some confession to make that may relieve his mind, and may be requisite for you to hear.

BARON. Well, bring him in, and do you wait in the adjoining room, till our conference is over. I must then, Sir, have a conference with you.

ANHALT. I shall obey your commands. [He goes to door, and re-enters with Frederick. Anhalt then retires at the same door.]

BARON [haughtily to Frederick]. I know, young man, you plead your mother's wants in excuse for an act of desperation: but powerful as this plea might be in palliation of a fault, it cannot extenuate a crime like yours.

FREDERICK. I have a plea for my conduct even more powerful than a mother's wants.

BARON. What's that?

FREDERICK. My father's cruelty.

BARON. You have a father then?

FREDERICK. I have, and a rich one—Nay, one that's reputed virtuous, and honourable. A great man, possessing estates and patronage in abundance; much esteemed at court, and beloved by his tenants; kind, benevolent, honest, generous—

BARON. And with all those great qualities, abandons you?

FREDERICK. He does, with all the qualities I mention.

BARON. Your father may do right; a dissipated, desperate youth, whom kindness cannot draw from vicious habits, severity may.

FREDERICK. You are mistaken—My father does not discard me for my vices—He does not know me—has never seen me—He abandoned me, even before I was born.

BARON. What do you say?

FREDERICK. The tears of my mother are all that I inherit from my father. Never has he protected or supported me—never protected her.

BARON. Why don't you apply to his relations?

FREDERICK. They disown me, too—I am, they say, related to no one—All the world disclaim me, except my mother—and there again, I have to thank my father.

BARON. How so?

FREDERICK. Because I am an illegitimate son. —My seduced mother has brought me up in patient misery. Industry enabled her to give me an education; but the days of my youth commenced with hardship, sorrow, and danger. —My companions lived happy around me, and had a pleasing prospect in their view, while bread and water only were my food, and no hopes joined to sweeten it. But my father felt not that!

BARON [to himself]. He touches my heart.

FREDERICK. After five years' absence from my mother, I returned this very day, and found her dying in the streets for want—Not even a hut to shelter her, or a pallet of straw—But my father, he feels not that! He lives in a palace, sleeps on the softest down, enjoys all the luxuries of the great; and when he dies, a funeral sermon will praise his great benevolence, his Christian charities.

BARON [greatly agitated]. What os your father's name?

FREDERICK. —He took advantage of an innocent young woman, gained her affection by flattery and false promises; gave life to an unfortunate being, who was on the point of murdering his father.

BARON [shuddering]. Who is he?

FREDERICK. Baron Wildenhaim.

    [The Baron's emotion expresses the sense of amazement,
    guilt, shame, and horror.]

Lover's Vows

FREDERICK. In this house did you rob my mother of her honour; ; and in this house I am a sacrifice for the crime. I am your prisoner—I will not be free—I am a robber—I give myself up. —You *shall* deliver me into the hands of justice—You shall accompany me to the spot of public execution. You shall hear in vain the chaplain's consolation and injunctions. You shall find how I, in despair, will, to the last moment, call for retribution on my father.

BARON. Stop! Be pacified—

FREDERICK. —And when you turn your head from my extended corse, you will behold my weeping mother—Need I paint how her eyes will greet you?

BARON. Desist—barbarian, savage, stop!

Enter Anhalt alarmed.

ANHALT. What do I hear? What is this? Young man, I hope you have not made a second attempt.

FREDERICK. Yes; I have done what it was your place to do. I have made a sinner tremble [points to the Baron and exit.]

ANHALT. What can this mean? —I do not comprehend—

BARON. He is my son! —He is my son! —Go, Anhalt, —advise me—help me—Go to the poor woman, his mother—He can show you the way—make haste—speed to protect her—

ANHALT. But what am I to——

BARON. Go. —Your heart will tell you how to act. [Exit Anhalt.] [Baron distractedly.] Who am I? What am I? Mad—raving—no—I have a son—A son! The bravest—I will—I must—oh! [with tenderness.] Why have I not embraced him yet? [increasing his voice.] why not pressed him to my heart? Ah! see—[looking after him]—He flies from the castle—Who's there? Where are my attendants? [Enter two servants]. Follow him—bring the prisoner back. —But observe my command—treat him with respect—treat him as my son—and your master. [Exit.

END ACT IV.

ACT V.

SCENE I. Inside of the Cottage (as in Act II).

AGATHA, COTTAGER, and his WIFE discovered.

AGATHA. Pray look and see if he is coming.

COTTAGER. It is of no use. I have been in the road; have looked up and down; but neither see nor hear any thing of him.

WIFE. Have a little patience.

AGATHA. I wish you would step out once more—I think he cannot be far off.

COTTAGER. I will; I will go. [Exit.

WIFE. If your son knew what heaven had sent you, he would be here very soon.

AGATHA. I feel so anxious——

WIFE. But why? I should think a purse of gold, such as you have received, would make any body easy.

AGATHA. Where can he be so long? He has been gone four hours. Some ill must have befallen him.

WIFE. It is still broad day-light—don't think of any danger. —This evening we must all be merry. I'll prepare the supper. What a good gentleman our Baron must be! I am sorry I ever spoke a word against him.

AGATHA. How did he know I was here?

WIFE. Heaven only can tell. The servant that brought the money was very secret.

AGATHA [to herself]. I am astonished! I wonder! Oh! surely he has been informed—Why else should he have sent so much money?

56

Re-enter Cottager.

AGATHA. Well! —not yet!

COTTAGER. I might look till I am blind for him—but I saw our new Rector coming along the road; he calls in sometimes. May be, he will this evening.

WIFE. He is a very good gentleman; pays great attention to his parishioners; and where he can assist the poor, he is always ready.

Enter Mr. ANHALT.

ANHALT. Good evening, friends.

BOTH. Thank you, reverend Sir.

[They both run to fetch him a chair].

ANHALT. I thank you, good people—I see you have a stranger here.

COTTAGER. Yes, your Reverence; it is a poor sick woman, whom I took in doors.

ANHALT. You will be rewarded for it. [to Agatha.] May I beg leave to ask your name?

AGATHA. Ah! If we were alone— —

ANHALT. Good neighbours, will you leave us alone for a few minutes? I have something to say to this poor woman.

COTTAGER. Wife, do you hear? Come along with me. [Exeunt Cottager and his Wife.]

ANHALT. Now— —

AGATHA. Before I tell you who I am, what I am, and what I was— —I must beg to ask— —Are you of this country?

ANHALT. No—I was born in Alsace.

AGATHA. Did you know the late rector personally, whom you have succeeded?

ANHALT. No.

AGATHA. Then you are not acquainted with my narrative?

ANHALT. Should I find you to be the person whom I have long been in search of, your history is not altogether unknown to me.

AGATHA. "That you have been in search of! " Who gave you such a commission?

ANHALT. A man, who, if it so prove, is much concerned for your misfortunes.

AGATHA. How? Oh, Sir! tell me quickly—Whom do you think to find in me?

ANHALT. Agatha Friburg.

AGATHA. Yes, I am that unfortunate woman; and the man who pretends to take concern in my misfortunes is——Baron Wildenhaim——he who betrayed me, abandoned me and my child, and killed my parents. —He would now repair our sufferings with this purse of gold. [Takes out the purse.] Whatever may be your errand, Sir, whether to humble, or to protect me, it is alike indifferent. I therefore request you to take this money to him who sent it. Tell him, my honour has never been saleable. Tell him, destitute as I am, even indigence will not tempt me to accept charity from my seducer. He despised my heart—I despise his gold. —He has trampled on me—I trample on his representative. [Throws the purse on the ground.]

ANHALT. Be patient—I give you my word, that when the Baron sent this present to an unfortunate woman, for whom her son had supplicated, he did not know that woman was Agatha.

AGATHA. My son? what of my son?

ANHALT. Do not be alarmed—The Baron met with an affectionate son, who begged for his sick mother, and it affected him.

AGATHA. Begged of the Baron! of his father!

ANHALT. Yes; but they did not know each other; and the mother received the present on the son's account.

AGATHA. Did not know each other? Where is my son?

ANHALT. At the Castle.

AGATHA. And still unknown?

ANHALT. Now he is known—an explanation has taken place; —and I am sent here by the Baron, not to a stranger, but to Agatha Friburg—not with gold! his commission was—"do what your heart directs you. "

AGATHA. How is my Frederick? How did the Baron receive him?

ANHALT. I left him just in the moment the discovery was made. By this time your son is, perhaps, in the arms of his father.

AGATHA. Oh! is it possible that a man, who has been twenty years deaf to the voice of nature, should change so suddenly?

ANHALT. I do not mean to justify the Baron, but—he has loved you—and fear of his noble kindred alone caused his breach of faith to you.

AGATHA. But to desert me wholly and wed another—

ANHALT. War called him away—Wounded in the field, he was taken to the adjacent seat of a nobleman, whose only daughter, by anxious attention to his recovery, won his gratitude; and, influenced by the will of his worldly friends, he married. But no sooner was I received into the family, and admitted to his confidence, than he related to me your story; and at times would exclaim in anguish— "The proud imperious Baroness avenges the wrongs of my deserted Agatha. " Again, when he presented me this living, and I left France to take possession of it, his last words before we parted, were—"The moment you arrive at Wildenhaim, make all enquiries to find out my poor Agatha. " Every letter from him contained "Still, still, no tidings of my Agatha. " And fate ordained it should be so, till this fortunate day.

AGATHA. What you have said has made my heart overflow—where will this end?

ANHALT. I know not yet the Baron's intentions: but your sufferings demand immediate remedy: and one way only is left—Come with me to the castle. Do not start—you shall be concealed in my apartments till you are called for.

AGATHA. I go to the Baron's? —No.

ANHALT. Go for the sake of your son—reflect, that his fortunes may depend upon your presence.

AGATHA. And he is the only branch on which my hope still blossoms: the rest are withered. —I will forget my wrongs as a woman, if the Baron will atone to the mother—he shall have the woman's pardon, if he will merit the mother's thanks—[after a struggle]—I *will* go to the castle—for the sake of my Frederick, go even to his father. But where are my good host and hostess, that I may take leave, and thank them for their kindness?

ANHALT [taking up the purse which Agatha had thrown down]. Here, good friend! Good woman!

Enter the COTTAGER and his WIFE.

WIFE. Yes, yes, here I am.

ANHALT. Good people, I will take your guest with me. You have acted an honest part, and therefore receive this reward for your trouble. [He offers the purse to the Cottager, who puts it by, and turns away].

ANHALT [to the Wife]. Do *you* take it.

WIFE. I always obey my pastor. [taking it].

AGATHA. Good bye. [shaking hands with the Cottagers.] For your hospitality to me, may ye enjoy continued happiness.

COTTAGER. Fare you well—fare you well.

WIFE. If you find friends and get health, we won't trouble you to call on us again: but if you should fall sick or be in poverty, we shall take very unkind if we don't see you.

[Exeunt Agatha and Anhalt on one side, Cottager and his Wife on the other].

SCENE II. A Room in the Castle.

BARON sitting upon a sopha. —FREDERICK standing near him, with one hand pressed between his—the Baron rises.

BARON. Been in battle too! —I am glad to hear it. You have known hard services, but now they are over, and joy and happiness will succeed. —The reproach of your birth shall be removed, for I will acknowledge you my son, and heir to my estate.

FREDERICK. And my mother— —

BARON. She shall live in peace and affluence. Do you think I would leave your mother unprovided, unprotected? No! About a mile from this castle I have an estate called Weldendorf—there she shall live, and call her own whatever it produces. There she shall reign, and be sole mistress of the little paradise. There her past sufferings shall be changed to peace and tranquility. On a summer's morning, we, my son, will ride to visit her; pass a day, a week with her; and in this social intercourse time will glide pleasantly.

FREDERICK. And, pray, my Lord—under what name is my mother to live then?

BARON [confused]. How?

FREDERICK. In what capacity? —As your domestic—or as— —

BARON. That we will settle afterwards.

FREDERICK. Will you allow me, Sir, to leave the room a little while, that you may have leisure to consider *now*?

BARON. I do not know how to explain myself in respect to your mother more than I have done already.

FREDERICK. My fate, whatever it may be, shall never part me from her. This is my firm resolution, upon which I call Heaven to witness! My Lord, it must be Frederick of Wildenhaim, and Agatha of Wildenhaim—or Agatha Friburg, and Frederick Friburg. [Exit.

BARON. Young man! Frederick! —[calling after him.] Hasty indeed! would make conditions with his father. No, no, that must not be. I just now thought how well I had arranged my plans—had relieved my heart of every burden, when, a second time, he throws a mountain upon it. Stop, friend conscience, why do you take his part? —For twenty years thus you have used me, and been my torture.

Enter Mr. ANHALT.

Ah! Anhalt, I am glad you are come. My conscience and myself are at variance.

ANHALT. Your conscience is in the right.

BARON. You don't know yet what the quarrel is.

ANHALT. Conscience is always right—because it never speaks unless it *is* so.

BARON. Ay, a man of your order can more easily attend to its whispers, than an old warrior. The sound of cannon has made him hard of hearing. —I have found my son again, Mr. Anhalt, a fine, brave young man—I mean to make him my heir—Am I in the right?

ANHALT. Perfectly.

BARON. And his mother shall live in happiness—My estate, Weldendorf, shall be hers—I'll give it to her, and she shall make it her residence. Don't I do right?

ANHALT. No.

BARON [surprized]. No? And what else should I do?

ANHALT [forcibly]. Marry her.

BARON [starting]. I marry her!

ANHALT. Baron Wildenhaim is a man who will not act inconsistently. —As this is my opinion, I expect your reasons, if you do not.

BARON. Would you have me marry a beggar?

ANHALT [after a pause]. Is that your only objection?

BARON [confused]. I have more—many more.

ANHALT. May I beg to know them likewise?

BARON. My birth!

ANHALT. Go on.

BARON. My relations would despise me.

ANHALT. Go on.

BARON [in anger]. 'Sdeath! are not these reasons enough? —I know no other.

ANHALT. Now, then, it is my turn to state mine for the advice I have given you. But first, I must presume to ask a few questions. — Did Agatha, through artful insinuation, gain your affection? or did she give you cause to suppose her inconstant?

BARON. Neither—but for me, she was always virtuous and good.

ANHALT. Did it cost you trouble and earnest entreaty to make her otherwise?

BARON [angrily]. Yes.

ANHALT. You pledged your honour?

BARON [confused]. Yes.

ANHALT. Called God to witness?

BARON [more confused]. Yes.

ANHALT. The witness you called at that time was the Being who sees you now. What you gave in pledge was your honour, which you must redeem. Therefore thank Heaven that it is in your *power* to redeem it. By marrying Agatha the ransom's made: and she brings a dower greater than any princess can bestow—peace to your conscience. If you then esteem the value of this portion, you will not hesitate a moment to exclaim, —Friends, wish me joy, I will marry Agatha.

[Baron, in great agitation, walks backwards and forwards, then takes Anhalt by the hand.]

BARON. "Friend, wish me joy—I will *marry* Agatha. "

ANHALT. I do wish you joy.

BARON. Where is she?

ANHALT. In the castle—in my apartments here—I conducted her through the garden, to avoid curiosity.

BARON. Well, then, this is the wedding-day. This very evening you shall give us your blessing.

ANHALT. Not so soon, not so private. The whole village was witness of Agatha's shame—the whole village must be witness of Agatha's re-established honour. Do you consent to this?

BARON. I do.

ANHALT. Now the quarrel is decided. Now is your conscience quiet?

BARON. As quiet as an infant's. I only wish the first interview was over.

ANHALT. Compose yourself. Agatha's heart is to be your judge.

Enter AMELIA.

BARON. Amelia, you have a brother.

AMELIA. I have just heard so, my Lord; and rejoice to find the news confirmed by you.

BARON. I know, my dear Amelia, I can repay you for the loss of Count Cassel; but what return can I make to you for the loss of half your fortune?

Lover's Vows

AMELIA. My brother's love will be ample recompense.

BARON. I will reward you better. Mr. Anhalt, the battle I have just
fought, I owe to myself: the victory I gained, I owe to you. A man of
your principles, at once a teacher and an example of virtue, exalts his
rank in life to a level with the noblest family—and I shall be proud to
receive you as my son.

ANHALT [falling on his knees, and taking the Baron's hand]. My
Lord, you overwhelm me with confusion, as well as with joy.

BARON. My obligations to you are infinite—Amelia shall pay the
debt. [Gives her to him.]

AMELIA. Oh, my dear father! [embracing the Baron] what blessings
have you bestowed on me in one day. [to Anhalt.] I will be your
scholar still, and use more diligence than ever to please my *master*.

ANHALT. His present happiness admits of no addition.

BARON. Nor does mine—And yet there is another task to perform
that will require more fortitude, more courage, than this has done! A
trial that! —[bursts into tears]—I cannot prevent them—Let me—let
me—A few minutes will bring me to myself—Where is Agatha?

ANHALT. I will go, and fetch her. [Exit Anhalt at an upper entrance.]

BARON. Stop! Let me first recover a little. [Walks up and down,
sighing bitterly—looks at the door through which Anhalt left the
room.] That door she will come from—That was once the dressing-
room of my mother—From that door I have seen her come many
times—have been delighted with her lovely smiles—How shall I
now behold her altered looks! Frederick must be my mediator. —
Where is he? Where is my son? —Now I am ready—my heart is
prepared to receive her—Haste! haste! Bring her in.

> [He looks stedfastly at the door—Anhalt leads on
> Agatha—The Baron runs and clasps her in his arms—
> Supported by him, she sinks on a chair which Amelia
> places in the middle of the stage—The Baron kneels by her
> side, holding her hand.]

BARON. Agatha, Agatha, do you know this voice?

66

Lover's Vows

AGATHA. Wildenhaim.

BARON. Can you forgive me?

AGATHA. I forgive you. [embracing him].

FREDERICK [as he enters]. I hear the voice of my mother! —Ha! mother! father!

> [Frederick throws himself on his knees by the other side of his mother—She clasps him in her arms. —Amelia is placed on the side of her father attentively viewing Agatha—Anhalt stands on the side of Frederick with his hands gratefully raised to Heaven.]——The curtain slowly drops.

END.

EPILOGUE.

WRITTEN BY THOMAS PALMER, ESQ.
OF THE TEMPLE.

SPOKEN BY MR. MUNDEN.

OUR Drama now ended, I'll take up your time
Just a moment or two in defence of my *rhime*
  * "Tho' I hope that among you are *some* who *admir'd*
  "What I've hitherto said, dare I hope none are tir'd?
  "But whether ye have, or have not heard enough
  "Or whether nice critics will think it all stuff;
  "To myself *rhime* has ever appear'd, I must own,
  "In its nature a sort of *philosopher's stone*;
  "And if Chymists wou'd use it, they'd not make a pother,
  "And puzzle their brains to find out any other."
Indeed 'tis most strange and surprising to me
That all folks in *rhiming* their int'rest can't see;
For I'm sure if it's use were quite common with men,
The world would roll on just as pleasant again.
  "'Tis said, that while ORPHEUS was striking his lyre,
  "Trees and brutes danc'd along to the sound of the wire;
  "That AMPHION to walls soon converted the glebes,
  "And they rose, as he sung, to a city call'd Thebes;
  "I suppose *they* were *Butlers* (like me) of that time,
  "And the tale shows our sires knew the wonders of *rhime*."
From time immemorial, your lovers, we find,
When their mistresses' hearts have been proud and unkind,
Have resorted to *rhime*; and indeed it appears
That a *rhime* would do more than a bucket of tears.
Of love, from experience, I speak— odds my life!
I shall never forget how I courted my wife:
She had offers in plenty; but always stood neuter
'Till I, with my pen, started forth as a suitor;
Yet made I no mean present of *ribband* or *bonnet*,
My present was caught from the stars—'twas a *sonnet*.
  "And now you know this, sure 'tis needless to say,
  "That prose was neglected, and *rhime* won the day—
  "But its potent effects you as well may discover
  "In the *husband* and *wife*, as in *mistress* and *lover*;
  "There are some of ye here, who, like me, I conjecture.

Lover's Vows

"Have been lull'd into sleep by a good *curtain lecture*.
"But that's a mere trifle; you'll ne'er come to blows,
"If you'll only avoid that dull enemy, *prose*.
"Adopt, then, my plan, and the very next time,
"That in words you fall out, let them fall into *rhime*;
"Thus your sharpest disputes will conclude very soon,
"And from jangling to jingling you'll chime into *tune*.
"If my wife were to call me a *drunken old sot*,
"I shou'd merely just ask her, what Butler is not?
"And bid her take care that she don't go to pot.
"So our squabbles continue a very short season,
"If she yields to my *rhime*—I allow she has reason."
Independent of this I conceive *rhime* has weight
In the higher employments of church and of state,
And would in my mind such advantages draw,
'Tis a pity that *rhime* is not sanctioned by law;
  "For 'twould *really* be serving us all, to impose
  "A capital fine on a man who spoke prose."
Mark the pleader who clacks, in his client's behalf,
His technical stuff for three hours and a half;
Or the fellow who tells you a long stupid story
And over and over the same lays before ye;
Or the member who raves till the whole house are dosing.
What d'ye say of such men? Why you say they are prosing.
So, of course, then, if *prose* is so tedious a *crime*,
It of consequence follows, there's *virtue* in *rhime*.
The best piece of prose that I've heard a long while,
Is what gallant Nelson has sent from THE NILE.
And had he but told us the story in *rhime*,
What a thing 'twou'd be; but, perhaps, he'd no time.
So, I'll do it myself—Oh! 'tis glorious news!
Nine *sail* of the line! Just a ship for each Muse.
As I live, there's an end of the French and their navy—
Sir John Warren has sent the Brest fleet to Old Davy.
'Tis in the Gazette, and that, every one knows,
Is sure to be truth, tho' 'tis written in prose.

Printed in the United Kingdom
by Lightning Source UK Ltd.
126762UK00001B/308/A